A, B, See Colorado

An Alphabet Book of the Centennial State

Claudia Cangilla McAdam

Photography by **John Fielder**

For my educator-sisters,
Linda, Kathy, and Patti,
and for teachers and librarians everywhere.

Claudia Cangilla McAdam

I dedicate this book to
Virginia Carolyn Visser, little Gigi,
the reincarnation of her grandmother.

John Fielder

Text: © 2012 Claudia Cangilla McAdam. All rights reserved.
Photography: © 2012 John Fielder. All rights reserved.

Spot Illustrations, Map, and Book Design: Anna-Maria Crum

Published by:
John Fielder Publishing
P. O. Box 26890
Silverthorne, CO 80497-6890
www.johnfielder.com

Printed in the U.S.A. by Bang Printing

CURRENT PRINTING (last digit)
10 9 8 7 6 5 4 3 2 1

Library of Congress Control Number: 2012904200

Publisher's Cataloging-in-Publication Data

McAdam, Claudia Cangilla
  A, B, See Colorado by Claudia Cangilla McAdam; photography by John Fielder
  32 p.

Summary: A presentation of information about Colorado locations in an alphabetical arrangement and featuring photography of Colorado. Includes a map and location identifiers, a glossary, and associated learning activities.

ISBN 978-0-9860004-0-9

1. Colorado-Juvenile literature. 2. English language-Alphabet-Juvenile literature.

One of the best things about Colorado is the stunning scenery of the state, from the expansive Eastern Plains to the snow-capped tips of the Rocky Mountains to the sculpted hills of the Great Sand Dunes. Through photos that span the state and cover all four seasons, and with poetic descriptions that bring each scene to life, this unique alphabet book is a celebration of the beauty and variety of Colorado's natural wonderland: the flora, the fauna, the grand panoramas, the picturesque details. The enchanting verse of children's author Claudia Cangilla McAdam and the spectacular photography of John Fielder combine to take children of all ages on a captivating lyrical and pictorial journey around Colorado from A to Z.

—John Hickenlooper, Governor of Colorado

A, B, See Colorado is the third children's book collaboration by author Claudia Cangilla McAdam and photographer John Fielder. Their previous kids' books are **Do You See What I See?** and **Maria's Mysterious Mission**. To learn more about these books as well as Claudia's and John's individual works, please visit their respective web sites:

www.claudiamcadam.com
and www.johnfielder.com.

For more information about books and calendars published by John Fielder Publishing, please contact your local bookstore, web retailer, John Fielder's Colorado Gallery (303-744-7979), or visit johnfielder.com. Book resellers please contact Books West distributors at bookswest.net

Rattlesnake Canyon Arch, Black Ridge Canyons Wilderness near Grand Junction

Arches carved by nature's knife

Bluebells bursting into life

Gore Range Creek, Eagles Nest Wilderness near Silverthorne

San Juan Mountains

Columbines, the blooms of state

Deer tracks

cloven hooves

create

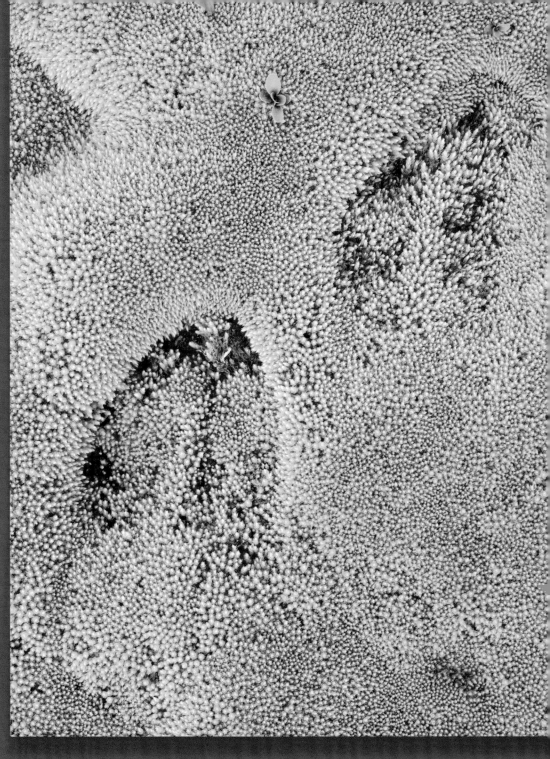

Rocky Mountain National Park

Rocky Mountain National Park

Elk herd standing tall with pride

Fox pups posing side-by-side

Greenwood Village

Mayflower Gulch Mine near Copper Mountain

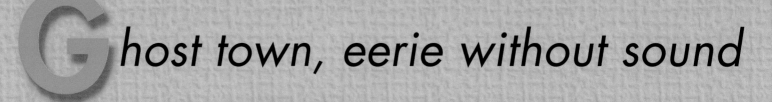

Ghost town, eerie without sound

Hay bales scattered on the ground

San Luis Valley below the Sangre de Cristo Mountains near Alamosa

Williams Fork Mountains

cicles, sharp frozen quills

Jagged Mountain— hiking thrills

Jagged Mountain, Weminuche Wilderness, San Juan Mountains

Hovenweep National Monument near Cortez

Kingdom crumbled long ago

Aspen Meadow, San Juan Mountains

Leaves ablaze with aspen glow

Gore Range, Eagles Nest Wilderness near Vail

Mountains scraping sunrise skies

Needles snagging autumn's prize

Gunnison National Forest

Dolores River Overlook, Southwestern Colorado

Overlook from cliffside throne

Escalante Ranch, Escalante Canyon, Delta County

Petroglyphs etched into stone

Queen's Crown flowers, pinkish-red

Rocky Mountain National Park

Focus Ranch along Little Snake River in Routt County

Rainbow's stunning, showy spread

Sunset stripes smeared 'cross the sky

Uncompahgre Plateau near Grand Junction

Eastern Colorado

Thunderstorm in hot July

Uncompahgre* vast plateau

*un-kum-**pah**-gree

Grand Mesa, Uncompahgre Plateau near Grand Junction

Ruby Range, Raggeds Wilderness near Crested Butte

Vista painted white with snow

Cascade Creek, San Juan Mountains

Waterfall of misting spray

Xeriscape*

done nature's way

Pawnee Buttes, Pawnee National Grassland, Northeastern Colorado

Yampa River far below

Yampa River near Steamboat Springs

East River, Gunnison National Forest near Crested Butte

Zig-zags formed by gentle flow

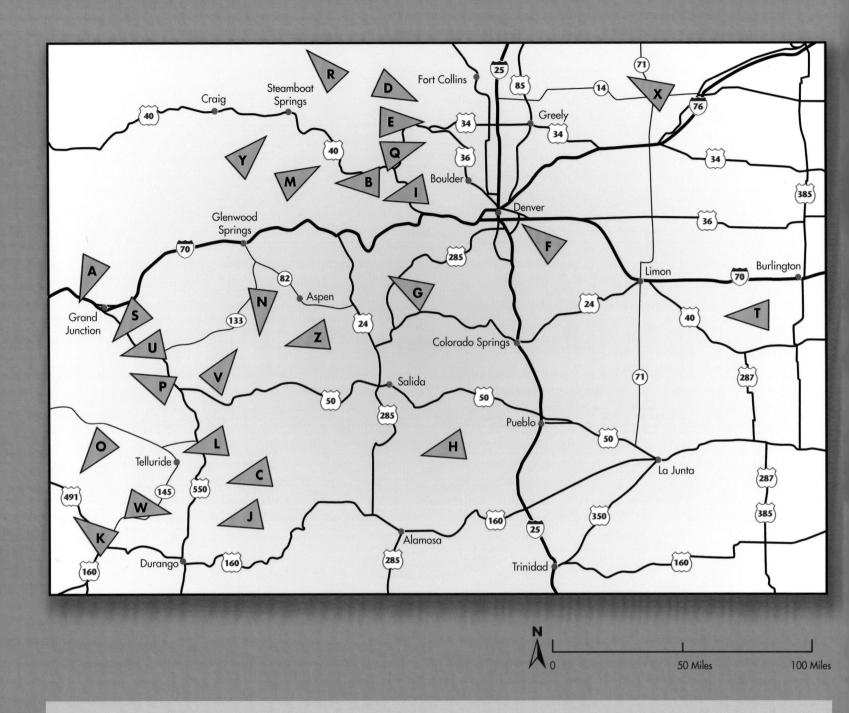

E Rocky Mountain National Park
Trail Ridge Road runs through the park, and at an elevation of 12,183 feet, it is the highest continuous highway in the U.S. One-third of the park is above timberline.

F Greenwood Village

G Mayflower Gulch Mine near Copper Mountain
Between 1928 and 1947, the Mayflower produced over 341,000 ounces of gold, 4.9 million ounces of silver, and 34,000 tons of lead, zinc, and copper.

H San Luis Valley below the Sangre de Cristo Mountains near Alamosa

I Williams Fork Mountains

J Jagged Mountain, Weminuche Wilderness, San Juan Mountains

K Hovenweep National Monument near Cortez
Humans lived at Hovenweep (a word meaning "Deserted Valley") as early as 10,000 years ago. Farming people lived in the area from about 500 A.D. to 1300 A.D. The towers at Hovenweep were built between 1200 and 1300 A.D.

L Aspen Meadow, San Juan Mountains
Large groupings of aspen trees are called "stands," and they are formed through root sprouts coming off an original parent tree, making them among the largest organisms in the world, by mass or volume.

M Gore Range, Eagles Nest Wilderness near Vail

N Gunnison National Forest

O Dolores River Overlook, Southwestern Colorado
The full Spanish name given the river in 1776 was "Río de Nuestra Senora de los Dolores" or "River of Our Lady of Sorrows."

P Escalante Ranch, Escalante Canyon, Delta County
In August, 1776, a Spanish Franciscan missionary-explorer by the name of Father Silvestre Vélez de Escalante found the ancient ruins of a small Indian village in western Colorado, which he noted in his journal – the first written record of a prehistoric Anasazi site in Colorado.

Q Rocky Mountain National Park

R Focus Ranch along Little Snake River in Routt County

S Uncompahgre Plateau near Grand Junction
The name "Uncompahgre" comes from the Ute Indian word with many meanings describing water: "rocks made red by water," "rocks that make red water," or just "dirty water."

T Eastern Colorado

U Grand Mesa, Uncompahgre Plateau near Grand Junction

V Ruby Range, Raggeds Wilderness near Crested Butte

W Cascade Creek, San Juan Mountains

X Pawnee Buttes, Pawnee National Grassland, Northeastern Colorado
Thousands of frontier families came west to the grasslands to farm in the late 1800s, but droughts and harsh weather made growing crops difficult. Today, the area is 300 square miles of picturesque grassy plains and wide-open skies.

Y Yampa River near Steamboat Springs

Z East River, Gunnison National Forest near Crested Butte

GLOSSARY

ablaze: a·blaze [uh-**bleyz**] being on fire

centennial: cen·ten·ni·al [sen-**ten**-ee-uhl] pertaining to a 100th anniversary. Colorado is called the "Centennial State" because it was admitted to the Union in 1876, one hundred years after the signing of the nation's Declaration of Independence.

cloven: clo·ven [**kloh**-vuhn] split or divided in two

eerie: ee·rie [**eer**-ee] mysterious, strange, creepy, or frightening

hooves: hooves [hoovz] plural of hoof, the foot of a horse, donkey, deer, etc.

jagged: jag·ged [**jag**-id] having a sharply uneven edge or surface

petroglyph: pet·ro·glyph [**pe**-truh-glif] a carving or drawing on rock, especially one made by prehistoric people

plateau: pla·teau [pla-**toh**] an area of fairly level high ground

quill: quill [kwil] the hollow shaft of a feather or a long, thin sharp object that grows from the body of a porcupine or some other animals

Uncompahgre: un·com·pah·gre [un-kum-**pah**-gree] a Ute Indian word meaning "rocks made red by water," "rocks that make red water," or just "dirty water"

vista: vis·ta [**vis**-tuh] a view, especially a splendid view from a high position

xeriscape: xe·ri·scape [**zeer**-i-skeyp] a way to landscape a yard with plants that don't need a lot of water

LEARNING ACTIVITIES

- Take a letter of the alphabet and research things in Colorado that begin with that letter, for example, for "B"—bear, Boulder, beaver, big horn elk, buttes, Breckenridge, etc.

- Make your own petroglyph art project. Crumple up a paper bag or brown butcher's paper and soak it in water, then lay it flat to dry. When dry, it should look like old leather or the face of a cliff. Use a white crayon to draw on it some scenes from your life.

- Choose a photo from this book, research its location and write about the area, its history, etc.

- Use a camera or sketch pad to record things from A-Z in your neighborhood or town. Or, do pencil rubbings of things found outside: the sidewalk texture, leaves, bricks, and so on.

- Select a photo from this book and use it as a writing prompt for a narrative or a nonfiction piece.

FOR MORE INFORMATION

For more information about the state of Colorado and the locations shown in these photographs, see the web site links on the "Resources" page of the author's web site: www.claudiamcadam.com.